EVERY
DARK
WANING

EVERY
DARK
WANING

a
davida
jane

PLATYPUS PRESS, England

First edition, 2016

ISBN 978-0-9935321-3-9

Cover and interior layout by Peter Barnfather
Type set in Bergamo Pro, FontSite Inc.
Printed and bound in Great Britain by Clays Ltd, St Ives plc

Published by Platypus Press Limited

10 9 8 7 6 5 4 3 2 1

For Bess, who loved my words first.

I

II

III

I

[Severe Weather Warning]

The radio static in my brain
    plays on repeat.

There's never any music,
just the endless
sound of a station

    missing—

a place no train will find,
and a whistling wind that
burns up sleep.

Why can I only ever feel
my heart when it
    wants to stop beating?

I am a flood warning,
    an avalanche of
        hopelessness and sharp things

taped
together—

an attempt to build a raft,
that sunk before it ever reached the water.

[The Poet as a Man-Made Lake]

Craterous and sinking,
full to the depths with
what was left when other
people made choices—

I am the place in the universe
where something vital
went missing.

Drowning is defined
by submersion, a consumption
by the waves' heartbreak;

but nobody ever talks about
how you can be flooded in
your own skin,

not for lack of air, but
of lungs large enough
to swallow more oxygen
than the water you are
taking in—like a broken boat
on the surface, with
investments in the lake.

This is the life chosen
for you by those digging,
the landscaping of your
future, without a thought

that you might be afraid
of the water.

[The Praying Man]

a man, crouched,
bent over with dusty
knees, long worn from
begging; looking
up through the roof
and down at the ground,

with nothing
to offer God but
three shillings and
a mouth drenched
and dripping, soaked
to the bone; this
is what you see when
you enter the church.

he does not have
a name, nor do you
have one to give;
he would only lose
it again, like the others.

nothing belongs to
him but his spine,
perpetually curving
towards the pool
of moonlight on the
ground.

his face
is grey like the wind
whispering every one
of his unanswered
prayers to the heavens.

you see no god in
this church, but you see
him, crouching, bent over
with dusty knees
from kneeling on the
stone floor, screaming
loudly without any
words, and still,
no one answers.

[Arbores]

I am built with the
architecture of trees;
leaves upturned to the
sunlight and a spine that
curves with the wind.

Perennial ribcage rust,
acacia trees, and alders
with lemon-yellow catkins
draped across my neck like
a noose—hanging myself
in the breeze as the songbird
sings and the clouds waltz by.

Reaching up to the acrylic-
blue pooling above,
I know that if I grow
tall enough my hands
will come away stained
cerulean, with bird
feathers twisted around
my fingers and a half
moon stuck to one knuckle.

I'll kiss the velvet bruises
better, lick the paint
and taste the sky upon my lips.
The waves of grass below will
brush against my ankles (trying
desperately to catch my gaze), but
I won't even blink.

I'm far too busy looking up.

[The Scientific Facts of Sleeplessness]

The cityscape droops with the sunset,
and the whole world sinks into bruised, purple hues.
Our eyelids as heavy as the sky,
we struggle just to keep ourselves awake.

Bare legs entangled in dirty bed sheets
and a finger, tracing the line of my
coastline collarbone—
pulling me out to sea.

Our arms are full of sand
and weighing us down, down
to the ocean's bed;
to darkness.

The whole world is falling asleep,
but we're the sleepless city, the headlights
streaming on the highway,
the sunrise blinking the birds awake.

We are the apocalypse in an
already broken world,
and I'm too tired to spend any more time
seeking sleep.

[An Attempt at an Explanation]

Watch how the coastline
considers the ocean.
See how the sky peers
into the gaps between the stars,
struck by the depths of emptiness.

Do you understand, now?
This is how I speak: my words,
in any other form, come dripping
with tears and contradictions.

The poet is the most
honest part of me.

I can't quite manage it
when you ask if I'm okay.
You reveal me to the world,
rain clouds and all. *Are you sure*
you're not afraid of the flood?

I know, love, I'm not
making any sense.
It's hard to explain
when there's a storm inside
my ribs—

it's like this, see,
sometimes the moonlight gazes
into the starless parts of the sky,
and sees a
dark kind of nothing.

[Pink Sky]

too bad i can't breathe when my mouth opens to the rain, i get so full up of water that it only knows how to make tears. too bad this world only has a red sky at dawn because if it was red all the time i wouldn't need to bleed so much, i could just look up. there are so many motel rooms in my head, i let them out each night, but they've never even been lived in. if i had two hearts i would keep one for the warm girls and one for the ones with empty palms, who can't stop staring at the earth's belly imagining how they'd fit inside, who can't stop dreaming cocoons for themselves, so they can finally grow wings. last night i dreamed every star was a glowworm and we were living in an endless cavern, outside the real sky was bright pink and we never wanted to die.

[Upturned]

did you see them? clouds!
real clouds, underneath our
feet like the world's turned
upside down and we're
swimming in the sky with
the ocean above, dripping.

did you see the city lights?
like the night sky glittering
at the tips of our noses—
the earth so far below,
it didn't matter at all,

like the buildings were
museum walls to hang the
stars upon, like the moon above
was lamp-light illuminating
artwork for the lonely.

did you see me stare at
all of this with wonder?
eyes glowing in the face
of it all, mouth agape
and teeth glinting,
like they wanted to reach
out and take a bite.

did you see me tuck the
view into the back of my
mind, putting it away for a
cloudy day when the stars
aren't there and i can't think
of a reason to get out of bed.

today, i needed a reason
to get out of bed, and
the moon was the only thing
that came close.

[Apollo 11]

A rocket fired and a
breath taken, in unison;
two pointed gazes, tilted
up towards the night.

The stickiness of the
atmosphere traps in
all the words I never
wrote down, and the poet
in me flinches as I soar
into outer space.

Above, the moon watches with
a calm serenity the oceans
would deny, and the stars
scatter from the ship's path,
eager to avoid collision.

The poet starts counting
her breaths with her heartbeats,
one timer in each hand as she
writes (with ink
upon her tongue) across the
surface of the rock.

With no gravity to weigh
them down, her words float
into the sky; splaying across
the black like constellations,
and interfering with the
satellites, till they transmit
only poetry.

[Tell Me about the Moon]

A space station's silent
radio (at a loss for
what to say), you will
die three times before the
end of the day, and your
obituary will call you a tragedy.

The moon landing was fake, he says.
It wasn't one small step
for man, it was an earthquake,
a tremor back on earth,
it was every child's
dream coming true.

The astronaut would never
have been able to speak, he
would have fallen to tears, taken
one look at the magnificence
surrounding him, and his
heart would have stopped.

It was your death printed
thrice in the newspaper,
it was the notice growing
shorter and shorter as
the editor decided not to
waste the ink.

It was, *20-year-old, deceased,*
circumstances unknown,
family devastated.
It was nothing when
you think of how much
the moon meant to you.

By the time of your third death
you were feeling kind of tired,
you think you'd like it to stick
this time, but you look out
the window and there she is,
glinting in a pool of black.

You know this is not your
last death, your final stand,
your farewell tour, this
is just another small step,
this is just another fall.

[Long Distance]

How many years before the fire, how many years still
looking up to the night sky and seeing nothing but black.
How many years imagining a mirror, something we can
gaze into with wide eyes and see something that looks just
like us staring back, see creatures who, like us, have spent
their days looking up, all their days wondering whether
someone else was out there. Days hoping maybe, just
maybe, they weren't alone at all. How many days did we
dream up these people, dress them in bodies just like ours,
with lives shaped like ours, and words like ours—gave them
names that fit comfortably around our tongues, and then
extended our hands, outstretched, for them to shake. How
many times will we send our ships and crews for voyages
into the big blue, navigating around the stars to look for
some small hint that they're out there too. How many times
will we come back, shaking our heads in disappointment,
but with a glimmer in our eyes that says *we're not giving up
just yet*. How many days will we spend wasting away, raking
the galaxies just to prove we're not alone. Surely, we're not
alone out here.

[The House of Pindar]

This is a poem about sharp things—
like knives and words, and your
hands when you're sitting across
the table from me asking,
please just tell me what's wrong.

I am too sad to say. The words
get stuck in my throat, my insides
devouring each lilting syllable,
and by the time they reach
my mouth, there is nothing left.

You burn every house in me
but the poet's—raze them to
the ground and salt them so
they'll never grow back.
Only the writer remains.

The writer, with her trembling
heart, her trembling hands, and
a language in her lungs
that never quite makes it out,
except when turned into ink.

This is a poem about sharp things—
like eyes and teeth and the poet
you left standing while
everything else burned. And she still
loves you, even after all of this.

[A Study in Restoration]

This is all we are left with;
this is all we love with.
Let's rehearse putting our bones
back together, fitting jagged edge
into jagged edge and
tying it up with string.

I keep trying to build a dam—
I keep coming up rainstorm,
I keep coming up flood.

Empty my mind of water. I think,
surely a drought's better than drowning.

I'm writing a letter to the
bruises in the crooks of my elbows,
the ink is smudged, but you can still
make out the words, *I'm sorry. I'm sorry.*
I'm sending it via Heaven, so God
can add his own apology to the end.

We're a cracked window in the
wall of a haunted house.
Let's practice taping ourselves back
together for when we run out of forgiveness.

This looks like absolution,
which means first it must have looked like sin.

[Gilded Butterfly Bones]

we're all stumbling,
half blind and blue-lipped,
throats stained grey with
poetry.

will the great
Neptune's ocean
wash this ink
from our hands?

and we're all sipping paint
like dandelion wine,
drowning our
bones with colour,

but there's
never enough
poison
to go round.

II

[Quicksand]

Sinking:
    what it looks like
when somebody stops being alive
a little at a time.
    First, they lose their footing
on the ground,
       next, the
support of their ankles.
    Soon, their thrumming heart
    will disappear too, and
following that, their marble
neck and cheeks, lips, eyes
       nose, and ears. Lastly,
you will see their wrists,
often scarred, barely
hanging on.
    The wrists
are always the last to go,
and always
       the first
       to want it.

_....making]

here I am, managing
this deconstruction of self,
tearing away each delicate
layer from months and months
of grime and grinning and
lying about being okay.
here I stand, open, trying
to get back to what I was at
the beginning—which was?
nothing, an empty space,
a gap for lovers to peer through,
and try to steal a kiss, Pyramus
wooing the mulberry leaves.
here I am, seeing my face
bare for the first time in weeks,
seeing myself torn apart,
window panes ripped off and
left to rot, practicing the
best representation of self
I can manage. I will write
myself soft if I want to. I will
scream into the forest of
a lovely girl's throat if it helps
me sleep—and who are you
to tell me not to?

[The Highway Mirage]

In summer, we dance with
shoes off and sunglasses on, we turn
our heads at the sight of ourselves,
we tell everyone how glorious we
are—and walk like we mean it.

In summer, we lose the careful
tucked into our palms, we let
our wrists turn to sunlight
and flash smiles to the sky instead of
the sidewalk.

We breathe reckless abandon,
and nobody thinks of dying.

This is our life raft, our highway
to a helpline, our waiting room
at the psychiatrist's office—
in summer, we live like we're
alive and for once, we want to be.

In summer, we aren't sick.
But we still are, and autumn comes
with its browns and oranges and
worst of all, the blues. In the fall
we forget what it feels like to stand up.

[Dear Diary]

the time has come to create bad art—to throw
caution, not to the wind, but her younger brother,
and hope he catches it with his thin fingers and
practices consumption. we grow tired far more
easily than the ocean; she is always waving
but when you look over your shoulder, there's
no one there—is she waving to you? or perhaps,
the moon. there she sits, small as a stone
in the belly of a fish, swollen with pride, mouth
still gaping, her light shining on your face, but
you turn from the silver (you are chasing
gold)—with blue paint dripping down your fingers,
leaving accidental stains upon every gilded flower
you stop to admire. the dog you saw alone
on the street runs from you, and you know you're
a monster but cannot seem to stop.

you looked in a mirror once and saw only
a reflection of the sky above—with its grey, grey
clouds and the thunder screaming out in pain.
you are morning; a thin frost, and a shy sun
turning from you like a mother betrayed. the sky
forms the lid of your coffin and there is no more
digging to be done—your arms are made of aching,
your chest filled with grief, your shoulders were born
from the sound made when the heavens were
torn from the earth; when the winds were split
from their furious embrace, and the seas
became a mirror. you are no god. you have
no god, only a bird's wing caught by the wind.
you have no warmth, only a raw, raw heart.
it beats with a broken hum—a thunderclap
caught within a throat, you are trapped.

[The Nameless Thing]

We all have monsters
living in our lakes.

Sometimes they don't look
like monsters, they look like
smiles or good days or
other sweet things, but
they are monsters nonetheless.

This one is giant and dark,
a beast lurking in the deepest
depths. It tells me its name
every day, but I still refuse
to call it that.

Instead, it is the creature,
the sorrow, the darkness,
the hollow—the thing living
inside of me that makes me
want to die, even when I
am not myself.

I can see the creature in my eyes
when I look into the mirror, sleeping,
drowsing, turning everything
to silt and ash within me.
It doesn't mean any harm;

a quiet killing
is the nature of the beast.

[Nutritional]

my stomach hurts in
an empty, aching way, but
it doesn't want food,

(it doesn't want food)
(it doesn't want food)

it wants to devour the moon,
fill up, like a balloon
with a lake of water
glinting silver from the
giant clock face in the sky.

it wants to eat you whole,
taste your guts,
and your guilt, and the
grit in your teeth

and that day when you were
six years old and you fell
from a tree but you didn't cry—
you never cried.

[Dug up Stomach]

Gut spilling (pitted
against the world), empty
& howling, a bitter thing

you can always taste,
it calls & calls & calls,
but you can never give it what it wants.

Scare—a word that looks
almost like sacred but drops
into oblivion near the end,

something like hunger, something
like hiding, something like the letters
you address to your stomach on the worst nights

& the rest & every other day
in between. This is not a full moon
occasion, this is every dark waning—

constant, quaking, shaking hands
that refuse to let go of the heart,
to let go of starvation.

[The Starved]

This hollow hungry
ache in my gut,
asks for you.

It asks for the darkness.

I haven't bothered trying
to teach it how those are
very different things.

[When Your Home Is Not Your Home
  & Your Body Is Not Your Own]

this constant party trick;
making ourselves look lived in,

making our houses look like homes
(when we've never felt comfortable there),

making our faces look how faces
are expected to look (soft and friendly,

like a mirror, like everyone else),
making our arms look like open doors

and our sorrow like an apology note
(the envelope perfectly sealed),

making our breaths look less like
desperation and more like politeness,

like we're keeping ourselves alive
out of courtesy (like you don't

want me to die, but can't understand
why i have to act like this to live),

like safety means something other
than staying in bed.

you keep wanting to know if i'm safe,
you keep wanting to know if i feel

lived in, or if the resident
is looking after the place

(if she's polishing the silver, or
opening the curtains every day

so the neighbours feel welcome).
you keep wanting to know

if i treat my home the way you treat yours,
as if ours are anything alike.

you keep worrying that i'm tearing
down the drapes (to make room

for new things), but you've never lived
somewhere that didn't feel like home before,

you've never lived somewhere that
didn't feel lived in before.

[Depression as a Forest]

Growing aches, tiny blooms of bruises
constellated across the bricks, this
is some house you built with your carelessness.

The house stands still in the middle of a forest,
deep greens, and a terrible scream
once in a while when the birds pass by.

The trees have grown thicker since last month,
they have grown darker and taller and
the branches they bear carry more weight.

The knocking at the door grows louder
each day, but you never let the monsters in.
You already know every one of their names.

"Tomorrow," you think, *"Tomorrow I will*
pick this house up from its roots,
I will take the weight of it upon my shoulders."

"Tomorrow I will carry my aching frame
with the windows full of cobwebs and a leaky roof,
I will carry it out of these woods."

[War Chant]

the endless beat of a drum
behind your ears, tick-
tocking like a clock where the
second hand's winning

it's the
sound of your heartbeat, and your
mother's, and your sister's, and
all the ones before

the sound
of the marching—left-
right, left-right, black boots
through the streets, boarded
windows and screaming children

tick-tock, left-right, and
your heartbeat beats; can
you hear the ghosts singing—

[Halfway into the Lake]

I have been a ghost,

more rainstorm than person,
with stones sewn into
my skin and prison bars
wrapped around my bones.

And, it occurs to me
I have never been happy
even when I have.

Do you see? Sometimes
the weight of life becomes
unbearable,

is it the sadness
that makes the poet,
or the poet that makes
the sadness?

[Sunflowering]

this endless gold, this godless
field of aching—
 it wasn't built
 to be lived in.

you will find somewhere else
and call it *home*
and for once it will
 act like it:
take in deep, shaky breaths with
you, chest pressed against chest,

hands clasped, both
trying desperately to fill

the space inside of you with air
before the collapse. roof

to lungs, door to open palm
(you will feel holy there, and
even more, you will feel whole).

but, none of this is news,
you've been building this
nest in your veins for ten years,

it kept you company through
the worst times, and only you
can see the colours of the

window frames and
how high the ceilings are
and how big the flowerbeds.

how big are they? how big?
    your wide open heart,
your trembling hands trying to grow
something, anything, in the dirt
of your own pain (for so long),

    and now you can.

[Mortal Shoulders]

We could lie like this for
centuries; watch cities rise
and empires fall, watch stars die
and gods grow weary until
we are the only ones left.

I'm tired, love, I'm heavy with
exhaustion and I don't think
I can lift myself from this place.
My arms are filled with stones,
my bones weighed down with iron,
and my head holds the whole world
within it.

Atlas, lend me your arms.
I have not the strength to hold
myself up.

III

[You Found a Poet in the Forest]

You found a poet in the forest, you brought them home with dirt stuck to the soles of their feet and dying leaves nestled in their hair—you gave them an empty cage, their own key, and a secret door to yours. You handed your heart over willingly for a sonnet; the most expensive fourteen lines you'd ever heard.

You found a poet in the forest and fixed their messy hair and broken strings, you told them that they were too much for the world outside, that their words burned like the blood in your veins, told them love was eternal and they devoured it like poets do.

You found a poet in the forest and kept them as your own, and for sixteen days and sixteen nights they spun poem after poem until your house was made of paper and a love you could never be rid of.

You found a poet in the forest and they knew you would forget them. You found a poet in the forest and they left before you could turn them away, they disappeared (back among the trees and the shadows), and you were left with a hollowness in your gut and fragments of poetry scrawled upon your house.

[A Poem for Those Who Watch the Stars at 2am]

Star gazer, moon
raker—did you
place the galaxies
yourself?

Did you, with trembling hands,
press each bright seed
into the overturned earth
of the sky?

You look at them
as if you did
(with tired eyes and
a head full of stardust).

They are your
long lost lover;
your bursting heart and
the emptiness of your lungs.

[Glass Slipper Hearts]

i.

we are a pair of towers, keeping golden songbirds
and naked hearts locked inside. i am a wicked
witch, offering bones through the bars of a
cage made of ribs, and you have beasts aplenty.

ii.

we give up our voices as the night closes in,
burning ourselves on the last of the matches as
everything goes cold. our story is not one that
would grace the dark of a thousand and one
nights—nobody will look for our falling-star-
hearts in history, but still—

iii.

i'll follow the sound of your bleeding
even when i'm blind.

[Doorstep]

My heartbeat's flat-lining, a horizon
line of grey between my sky blues
and the ground. I can't go outside
without seeing ghosts in the rain,
and corpses in every doorway.

Stop standing on my doorstep when
you look half-dead, stop leaving me
standing here on yours.

Somebody stole my hands, they're
missing and I've nothing to lift myself
up with. I've been staring at the stars
for hours now, with no fingers to
point and whisper, *look*.

I wanted to introduce my ribcage
to the constellations, I feel they'd
get along; they both have gaps
in between where everything falls
through and nightmares hide.

In the morning when you leave,
you'll step over me, still sitting outside
your house, with empty wrists and
a broken-down heart. I'll drag
myself from your doorstep,

walk home with my shoelaces
untied, hoping I don't end up
back there again this evening.

[The Moon in the Lake]

the night she left i knew
the silver satellite disc (shivering

at the bottom of the lake) had willingly
sunk, with shimmering fish giving

kisses to her cheeks and the night
fishermen dreaming of love songs

gilded with light. trees were hands
clasped and i, the damp earth,

a wrist stained with everything
they hid from each other,

missing her eyes like shattered
glass and writing only love poems.

[Growing Pains]

stop biting your tongue,
stop wishing on ruined dandelions,
on falling stars,
on other broken things.

you've turned yourself into
a half-hearted song,
waiting at the side of the road
for your backbone to come and pick you up.

you're beating out a rhythm
of your own making,
tapping out a series of wishes
and wants and maybes—

and i wanted to give you the world,
but i knew you wouldn't take it
from anyone but
your own ink-stained hands.

[Star Curator]

There's a canvas on the wall with
your body spilled upon it, your face
like a moon, and your mouth,
a gash of red.

You're hanging on the wall
of a museum and all the people
walking by fall in love with your
brushstrokes.

Nobody ever asks your name,
and sometimes, when the curator leaves,
he forgets to let down the blinds
and you can see out through the windows.

You can see the vibrant city lights
and the shining stars in the sky, and
the moon, staring down at you, and she
looks just like your face.

[Ocean Song]

a tired rhythm,
    a song
missing half of its lyrics
with a melancholic beat;

you were born to this sound.

out-of-tune strings and a
    hollow note thrumming
    through your chest.

you could mistake it for
your heartbeat, but then, you
wouldn't sleep if you did.

grating teeth, chipped,
    stolen,
like the ribs inside
your chest as you take
    a breath,

paid for with an
empty space in which to keep
jars of bad dreams and
oddities, and the
       loneliness you collect,
       like shells every
time you visit the sea.

a shiver running along
your harp-string tendons,
playing your bright red,
       bleeding,
       poppy field
       war song,
in a high-pitched
harmony of wanting.

this song is the most
       important part of you,
the trees sway to it and
       the sea hands wave back
              and forth to the rhythm,

the weary tune, the salt-soaked
singing you were born to.

[The Longest Night]

when the stars tire, when the heavens
grow weary of storytelling, this is what we get—
goodbyes, repeating forever, a wound
that must keep healing, an awful, endless
night, not star-crossed, but lost in god's eyes,
terrible poems that must still be written,
flowers blooming in january, and the sun
forgetting to set (which sounds like love,
but feels like no such thing), i can't stop
shivering and we can see each other's
ribs, don't you wonder where our skin's
gone to tonight, it's like we burned it off
one another to get closer, but
you still seem so far away, i don't think
we should do this anymore, because
you're dangerous for me, you see
if i spend too long in anyone's arms,
i start to call them home (and all your windows
are watching for someone who will never
come back), my mother would not be proud
of me today, but the days have not yet
forsaken me and your arms are built like wings
(tired from flight and shivering), this is no
arcadia, we will not rest well tonight,

and in the morning dawn, her sweet
mouth spreads pink across the sky, and
the flowers stretch their necks to catch
a glimpse of her, and we still will not rest.

[A Love Poem for an Imaginary Girl]

this is the story of a girl
who keeps her baby teeth
in a drawstring bag at the back
of her cupboard so she
never forgets her bite,

whose heart is a different
colour every month
(in january it's blue),
and whose mouth is like
a painter's mistake—

a sharp gash where they should
have used a softer brush,
jagged, like god's first
honest love poem, and
far too red to be real.

she sits in the broken light
of the dawn she's always
awake for, she sees
the sun rising and
isn't afraid.

[The Old Bicycle]

a stranger in a lake doesn't
seem so strange, especially
in december.

what did he take from you?
what did you give him?

there's a bicycle padlocked
to your front gate, rusted
and sinking in mud.

one morning you wake
and it's missing,
taken by a lonely thief
with somewhere
to go and no way to get there
and you wonder if
the old bike was enough.

that night, you come home
to an empty gate and the
white picket fence,
and a strange boy standing
in the pond amongst the lily pads—

not a stranger this time,
but just as unknowable.

[And Yes]

This is the dust you thought you'd
gotten rid of, thick across your shinbone,
seen through the gap in your armour.

Somebody asks if you're okay, and
you say *yes*. It's the only answer.
Yes, everything is fine. *Yes*, this is a lie.
Yes, I repeat the answer to myself
over and over though I'm meant to be
sleeping, and it still never sounds
like something I'm able to say aloud.

Yes, I love her. *Yes*, she knows.
Yes, sometimes I think about
how it will end, and *yes*, I can't stand it.
But *yes*, I can see the impending collapse,
the inevitable tunnel at the end of the light.

Yes, I know she sees it too. *Yes*,
we've talked about it. *Yes*, that makes it
so much worse, like now it's on paper
in an ink that will never fade—this
is not forever, no matter how much
I wish it was, no matter that I'd die
for it to be, and *yes*, I know that's
why it can't be. And it's why I'm
covered in dust, it's why there's
this gap in my armour in the first place,
because, I would die for so many things,
and she is one, but not having to think
about death is another.

[Love & Other Sweet Things We Expect Too Much Of]

An open mouth—your name,
written on it in ink or blood,
or something dark that
tastes bitter to the tongue.

Your hand on my wrist
is a lifeboat, and I am drowning
anyway, but at least you
keep me from doing it willingly.

Darling, did you know the
ache we feel is just our hearts hurting
from trying to beat at the same time.
Did you know that it hurts so much
because one time they got it right,
and every moment since has been
agony, a history of mistimed implosions
so desperately trying to be
together and never quite making it.

[Portrait of a Kiss]

in a sleepless night i dream her

collarbone is the edge of a ravine
i have failed to fall into, her hands,

willing anchors, and my heart, the
ocean bed—

and when i wake, the sky is burning,
and old sailors hang their heads while

painters take care to
leave all crimson hues to the sky,

and paint my mouth, curving into
hers, with only the softest pink.

[For Virginia]

the lake is no wholesome place. it holds
every door to every world but the one
you want to live in, it holds the key
to every love but the love of yourself,
it will sate every thirst but the thirst
for sanity. drink deep, and beside you
i will rest my head upon your shoulder,
and dream of panning for gold
in the broken shores of the world
like it could make up for everything
the sky has done to you. you have given
me hope that i am not alone, given me
a home in the balm of your words,
a shining beacon for every woman
who ever wanted to die, you have given
us a roof to live under. i hope you know
you are not alone. i stand on that roof
every day. my knees shake and my
hands tremble, but every day i build,
sewing tiles into the timeless fortress
you have pulled from the dirt—with hands
so soft and strong. we will keep building
until all the world is a home, with
so many open doors and one big window
where every young girl has a place to sit.

A. Davida Jane is a nineteen year old bisexual poet and aspiring novelist from Wellington, New Zealand. She studies English Literature and Classics at Victoria University, and hopes to continue those studies abroad in later years. Growing up she could always be found with a book in her hand, and now often a pen, but either way she is almost always thinking about words.

More of her work can be found at adavidajane.tumblr.com

[Acknowledgements]

I would firstly like to give thanks to the wonderful literary journals *The Rising Phoenix Review* and *–Ology Journal* who have previously published works of mine. I will always be grateful for those first opportunities to have my work published.

To Michelle and Peter at Platypus Press, I cannot say how thankful and how appreciative I am for everything you have done for me—to have this opportunity is a dream come true and that could never have happened without you, so thank you.

To my parents, I would firstly like to apologise. I know it's taken too long for you to be able to read these words of mine. I cannot thank you enough for always supporting me, and pushing me to reach for the stars and the moon and everything else. You taught me to love words, and so I hope you love mine.

For Steph, who is the best sister I could ever ask for. Thank you for always being there.

For Sarah and Darsh, who have never once stopped believing in me.

To Maddie, for being the most enthusiastic, encouraging, helpful, lovely cheerleader anyone's ever had—this book wouldn't exist without you.

Lastly, to my readers—your support and appreciation mean the world to me, and I only hope that my words can give you even half as much love back as you give me every day.

Check the Platypus Press website for further releases:

platypuspress.co.uk